CHARACTER
PLUS
COMMON SENSE

Management Principles for Success

A Simple Guide

Richard Sevcik

Character Plus Common Sense
Management Principles for Success
A Simple Guide
by Richard Sevcik

Printed in the United States of America

ISBN 9781615794553

www.xulonpress.com

CONTENTS

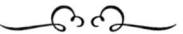

PREFACE

My objective in writing this book is to present the challenge of management in a simple fashion. Therefore, by definition this book is relatively short discussing five key management principles:

- ➤ Be Aggressive - Take Smart Risks
- ➤ Keep It Simple - As Simple As Possible
- ➤ Focus - And Focus Again
- ➤ Measure It - Or Don't Do It
- ➤ A Company Is Only As Good As The People.

I've always disliked long, complicated books on management. I believe that we need to utilize our common sense. I just don't believe management is that complicated when practiced correctly. However, I do understand that management is not easy; more on that later.

It's also true that not everyone can be a successful manager or leader. People management does require a certain set of character traits. These traits can be developed, if you put your mind to that task. I will discuss these character traits in the first two chapters of the book. Chapter one is devoted entirely to integrity, without which you will fail over the long run. Chapter two presents humor, openness, trust, and humility. Each of these traits will significantly enhance your management success.

I have devoted one chapter to each of the five key principles of successful management. Of course these principles do not each stand alone. They must be practiced in an integrated fashion. I've included a 'pyramid of success' on page xii as a visual reminder of all ten concepts presented in this book. If you check out my Facebook account, you will be able to down load the pyramid for your screen saver, as a constant reminder of the behavior that you are trying to establish. In addition I'd like to encourage you to document your focused objectives for each day as well as the current quarter. Include these objectives in your screen saver to help you stay focused.

As you read this book you may be wondering if these principles really work. I began to apply these principles at HP during the early nineties. Our computing business grew at a most impressive rate. Then I joined Xilinx in 1997. At that time Xilinx generated an annual revenue of $560 million. By the year 2006 the Xilinx revenue had increased to $1.7

billion with a net income in excess of 20%. This growth rate and profit were, and are, world class. As a result of this success the Xilinx market capitalization increased from $2.4 billion in 1997 to $8 billion in 2006. In addition to these wonderful financial results, Xilinx was also ranked in the FORTUNE Magazine's annual list of the "Top Ten Companies To Work For" for *four consecutive* years. These accomplishments were the result of a great team of people working together toward common goals.

In the appendix you can read an explanation of the Biblical basis for these key principles. As a Christian I find it very reassuring that God has revealed these principles for our use. I would encourage everyone to read the appendix. If you are unfamiliar with the Bible, I think you will find the appendix instructive.

Finally I would like to thank the numerous people who 'adopted' me during my career. They were my mentors. They cared about me - really cared! I would encourage each of you to look for someone in your life who is wiser than yourself, and ask them to 'adopt' you. Ask them to give you advice that you can embrace with open arms.

Numerous people have helped me in the final editing of this book. I would especially like to thank Bob Behrens, Bill Parkhurst, and T.J. Rodgers.

All of the profits from this book will be donated to several charities. They each provide help to disadvantaged people all across the United States and around the world.

As I write this book I would like to thank my wife, Charlene, who has been very patient with me. At times I really think that she is an angel.

INTRODUCTION

I decided to write this book because after thirty years of management experience, I believe that successful management is both simple (not complicated) and difficult (not easy). Management is simple because there are only a few, in my opinion five, common sense management principles that must be mastered on the job. But management is difficult because by human nature, we all tend to get distracted from these key principles. Maybe it's because at heart, we tend to be a bit lazy. But more likely, I think, we all tend to want to 'invent' as we go along in life. During a typical day at work, rather than follow principles, we want to get creative. To be sure creativity has its place at work, but it should not distract us from key fundamental principles. So excellence in management does require a great deal of focus to be successful. Focus is a habit that's not often taught anymore in our society. People think that they can do multiple things at the same time (surf

PYRAMID OF SUCCESS

– – –   SUCCESS   – – –

FOCUS

BE AGGRESSIVE

KEEP IT SIMPLE PLEASE

MEASURE IT — — OR DON'T DO IT

A COMPANY IS AS GOOD AS THE PEOPLE

– – – – – – – – – – – – – – – – – – – –

**INTEGRITY * TRUST * HUMILTY
OPENESS * HUMOR**

the web while speaking with someone or check email while attending a family gathering).

Also we can be repeatedly distracted by urgent interruptions. Nearly everybody and everything wants our attention, now. But we can't let these interruptions dominate our work day. We must set time aside to complete the work dictated by these key management principles. It's really all about personal focus. Excellence in management requires us to have the focus to manage our own creative distractions, and we must manage the external interruptions as well. That's why management is not easy.

By the way as you consider these management principles for yourself, be mindful of those who work with you in your group. It would be wise to expect them to practice these principles as well. In fact when hiring someone, these principles could be a check list for evaluating different candidates.

Before discussing these five common sense management principles, in Chapter one and two I will describe five key character traits that I believe are also instrumental for your success. Since all workers are human, there are style issues that can impact your management results in a very significant way. People can be attracted to you, or, repulsed by your style. These character traits are: integrity, humor, openness, trust, and humility. The more you can demonstrate these traits to fellow workers, the more likely it is that they will be attracted to you as a manager. And if they like you, they will usually be motivated to let you manage them. They will give you grace, instead of criticism. They will be attracted to your leadership. By the way these character traits can't be faked. For example you either have integrity or you don't. So don't try to fool fellow workers on these traits, it just will not work. In fact it will cause people to disdain you, making your management success nearly impossible.

I've devoted an entire chapter to the topic of integrity. I hesitate to call this a 'style' issue, but it's not a management principle either. Maybe, it's best thought of as a life principle, or simply a crucial character issue. Chapter 1 in many ways is the most critical chapter in this book. Integrity as a manager enables everything! In fact I believe that the great failing that we are experiencing today in government and financial institutions is due to a lack of integrity. It seems as though, everyday, the internet headlines are pointing out another high profile leader in America who has had a failing of integrity. They cheat and then try to defend themselves, usually not fooling anyone but themselves. Isn't it very interesting that in 1963 Martin Luther King Jr. said that he looked forward to a day when people will "… not be judged by the color of their skin, but by the content of their character…". Now, in 2009 after much progress has been made concerning racism, character is the trait that is sorely lacking. During these four decades it seems that we have lost the characteristic that Dr King was holding in highest esteem. Maybe we as a society must relearn that after all is said and done, honesty is the best policy. If people can't believe you, they will not follow you. Why should they?

Chapters 3 through 7 discuss each of the five key management principles. These principles are explained separately, but they must be practiced in an integrated fashion. Success depends upon the leverage they each gain from one another. In fact if one principle is practiced to the extreme, without balance from the others, success will be lacking.

I think that at the outset of this book it's appropriate to define success. There are of course many ways to think about success. Most people today would define it as the attainment of wealth and prestige. However, very often, the wealthy are not happy; in fact the wealthy tend to have the highest suicide rate in America. Success in life is a very deep subject. But for the purposes of this book, with its focus on management, I will define success as the achievement of your business goals. I would encourage you to set goals that will bring you prosperity, peace, and joy. In a work place context we are tempted to only focus on completing a successful project. But, your goals should also include good will for your team members. As I have grown older I have realized that successful projects come and go, but it's the people that are truly valuable. If your goals as a manager include the growth of your team members then you can expect many, many successful projects.

This book is written in a fashion that utilizes the word 'manager'. But in fact the principles presented in the book are applicable to any role of leadership. A leader is simply someone who strongly influences other people. You may be the leader of your family or the leader of your baseball team, and you will find these principles very useful. Or as an employee with no direct management responsibilities, you should consider yourself as a leader. Your employer is paying you to get a job done. As a leader you should determine the most effective way for your employer to get a great return on their investment in you. If you do that well you will soon receive recognition and reward for your leadership.

Finally for the purpose of clarity, here is a simple summary of this entire book.

> ➢ Always live and work with integrity; be honest with yourself and all the people whom you impact on a daily basis.
> ➢ Keep in mind that your character is on display at all times.
> ➢ Be intelligently aggressive in everything you do; remember that without risk there is usually little to gain.
> ➢ Always keep your products and your organization as simple as possible; it really does make life easier to live.

➤ Focus is crucial to getting things done quickly and successfully; it's often necessary to say "no" to a myriad of distractions.

➤ In business and in life set goals that are measurable, so you can know for sure that you are making progress.

➤ Always remember that people are your company's most valuable resource; and, that definitely includes you!

Chapter One

Integrity- Be Honest

KEY POINT: Always live and work with integrity; be honest with yourself and with all the people whom you impact on a daily basis.

Integrity is simply being honest. Say what you mean and mean what you say! Do what you say you will do. And, always be sure to speak what is on your heart with compassion. People are attracted to leaders who are sincere and do what they promise. It's become common place in our society to spin the truth to one's own convenience. To say different things to different audiences in order to make people happy with you, just doesn't work. That is not lasting happiness. People eventually figure you out, and when they do, they are definitely not happy with your lying. Politicians today seem to be learning this lesson the hard way, as evidenced by the current unpopularity of our members of Congress.

In addition, when speaking truth, compassion is of great value. Let's not unnecessarily hurt anyone's feelings. We can communicate the truth without adopting a brutally honest style. It's critical that you demonstrate sensitivity to the feelings of others, while simultaneously saying what is necessary. Early in my career one of my peers was a strong willed young manager (like myself). He and I would often have very brutal, honest conversations that only ended because our mutual boss would intervene after a painful hour or two. Well on one occasion our boss did not intervene, and that conversation nearly came to physical blows. We stopped *ourselves*; we learned to control ourselves out of respect for one another. From that day forward I learned that I am responsible for communicating honestly, and, with respect for my teammates.

EXAGGERATION

There is a great temptation in business to exaggerate and take credit for things that you did not really accomplish. It's all about making *me* look good, especially to the boss. It's sometimes called 'managing up', but it is a subtle form of lying. This is particularly damaging to teamwork. People will retaliate in kind when they feel that some else is trying to take credit that's due to their efforts. It makes everyone suspicious and puts them on alert. Of course, good teamwork is just the opposite. Teamwork happens when everyone is working for the good of the company and not taking credit for someone else's work. Think about it: if every person is doing what is best for the company, that is also what is best for each person. As a manager we must set the right example. Remember, people are watching you. Your team will do as you do. If you are exaggerating to your boss or teammates, they will eventually realize that's what you are doing to make yourself look good. This habit can't be sustained over time, because it must get more and more exaggerated to maintain the allusion of progress. Eventually the real, limited accomplishment is known to all. For example, in today's financial world, we have all become familiar with 'Ponzi' schemes. In this scheme the financial manager attempts to constantly promise bigger financial returns to his clients, but he in reality is secretively losing money. These schemes just can't last over a period of months or a few years. Often at the bitter end, the person who exaggerates is fired, and may even go to jail for breaking the law.

LYING

Then of course there is the possibility of blatantly lying, when it feels necessary. You are thinking that no one would do this! Oh really? Do people lie on their tax returns, or on company expense accounts, or in calculating corporate revenue, or in back

<u>INTEGRITY</u>

SAY WHAT YOU MEAN

MEAN WHAT YOU SAY

AND, JUST DO IT

####

REMEMBER PEOPLE ARE WATCHING YOU

####

THE GREATEST ABILITY IS DEPENDABILITY

dating stock options, etc.? Unfortunately many, many people do exactly that, as we all know from the news. This trend is getting worse. Forbes magazine recently documented that 90% of high school students admitted to cheating on tests; that's about triple the rate found in a survey conducted in 1963.[1] These high school students will eventually go to work and become managers. Will these managers be trust worthy?

And yes, I've had several managers outright lie to me. In one example I had signed a software cooperation contract with a partner company while I was employed at HP. Later that CEO failed to deliver anything specified in the contract, and he simply suggested that if we didn't like it we could sue him. Well, it wasn't worth the time or the cost of a law suit. So we cancelled the contract, and moved on with other business. That particular CEO was later fired for other illegal activities that he was found guilty of at his company. In addition he had also lied about his falsified college degrees. People who lie usually build a habit that they can't easily stop.

So I learned that professional people do lie. I have also learned that it's impossible to work with people like that. I never could know when I was hearing the truth. If you have someone like that on your team, you can never be sure what has really been accomplished or completed on a given task. Maybe they are exaggerating their results, or maybe the task is done but with poor quality. After all quality means attention to details, and just maybe the task was not really done properly, and now the person is misleading you. You don't want to have to manage a project while being suspicious about someone. And you certainly don't want to put your boss in that situation. Don't ever be so driven for success that you compromise your integrity. It's not worth it! In fact, it will not work over the long term anyway. Your lying will be discovered.

TEAMMATES

So my advice is: say what you mean and mean what you say. Secondly, my advice is: hire people with this style of integrity. In a recent management survey Information Week documented that ethics and morals have become the number one hiring criteria in the computer industry.[2] Unfortunately it's becoming very common for people to exaggerate, lie, and fail to live up to their commitments. If you commit to be somewhere, or do something, or deliver something; just do it. People are counting on you, and of course you are counting on other people. In fact one day I heard a wise man say: "The greatest ability is dependability".[3] Think about it! If people at work or at home can't count on your word, then managing well and gaining success is probably impossible.

I recently read about an interesting experiment in human psychology related to integrity.[4] In this particular experiment college students were presented with an opportunity to cheat on a test, and as a matter of fact, most of them did cheat repeatedly. However there was one group of students who were asked to write down as many of the Ten Commandments as they could recall. Immediately following their recall they were given the same opportunity to cheat as the first group. Amazingly none of the students in this second group cheated on the test. If we want to raise the level of integrity in our society, it would serve us well to simply teach the importance of integrity. In the very early years of the Ivy League colleges, integrity was routinely taught by the professors as an inherent part of many of the courses. It will positively serve our society if we encourage our citizens to speak the truth, always. This behavior is not a life style choice, but rather it is an imperative to a stable society.

Chapter Two

Character - Watch Your Style

KEY POINT: Keep in mind that your character is on display at all times.

Your style is how people perceive you. It's not mandatory, but as a manager it's very advantageous for people to like you and know that they can rely upon you. Being friendly and cordial really doesn't take that much energy and it will give you the benefit of the doubt with your team. After all, haven't you really appreciated bosses whom you liked to be with at work? But it's even more important that people know that they can trust you. It's ironic that Richard Nixon, in a commercial for Barry Goldwater in 1964, said the following: "With all the power that a President has, the most important thing to bear in mind is this: you must not give power to a man unless, above everything else, he has character. Character is the most important qualification the

President of the United States can have." Managers in most companies wield a large amount of power! With that imperative let's consider four more character traits of a great manager.

HUMILITY

Let's take a look at humility. This topic is one of my favorites because I struggle with it the most. In our society we are always told that "it's all about *me*". However, we all love to work with humble people rather than with arrogant people. A humble person is a person who just doesn't dwell on themselves. Humility does not imply that the person is boring or simple. People who are humble are more concerned with how you and the team are doing, rather than themselves. Humble people are easy to work with because we really like them. In fact in their humility they often build us up with their compliments. So each of us should be humble! Doesn't that make sense? Well, most of us are not humble. I think it's because we are afraid that other people, who are not humble, will take advantage of us in some way. But this fear results from an improper definition of humility. Many people think that being humble means to demean myself periodically, or to not represent myself well. Or, even worse, some people think that humility means that I should walk around with my head hanging down. Real humility is simply being yourself; no more and no less. That means that we admit to our limitations, and we are confident of our capabilities. So it's important that we know ourselves very well. Make a list of the things in which you are competent, and list the things in which you could improve. Ask people around you to help you complete the list. By the way if you don't want to ask others to help you with your list, you must not be humble. Also, it might be useful to do one list at your work place, and another with your family at home. I'm sure that your kids will want to help you with your list of needed improvements.

If you practice humility, very quickly, your team will follow in your footsteps. Your team will become more cohesive and supportive of one another. I saw this happen at Xilinx. Bernie Vonderschmitt, who was the Founder, quickly built a billion dollar company as a humble, customer and employee focused executive. As a result of Bernie's role model, Xilinx was always rated number one in customer service compared to our competitors. In another example Bill Hewlett and Dave Packard did the same thing as Founders of HP, and their legacy continues decades later. HP's customers and business partners still have a strong appreciation for the company's customer focused culture.

The opposite of course is very evident all around the world. CEO's who are arrogant and often quick tempered can destroy team work and the whole company. These CEO's often come to believe that they know more than they really do, and they often begin to think that they are above the law as well. Eventually reality does catch up with them, and unfortunately many people suffer. These companies will often take on the persona of their CEO to the detriment of the business.

The bottom line is that a humble manager is appreciated by their teammates, stock holders, and by their customers as well.

HUMOR

Let's move on to discuss humor. I'm not necessarily talking about someone who tells jokes. Stand-up comedy is not easy! I'm suggesting that, most of the time, you keep a light hearted attitude at work. It's best if people are feeling at ease with you; they are more likely to be themselves in your presence. On the other hand if you are always serious, demanding, or intense, that behavior will actually drain energy from people around you. They will feel like they have to keep their guard up to protect themselves from your tough attitude. That defensive mind set takes energy from people; wasted energy that instead could be used more productively!

When the opportunity arises, even poke fun at yourself. Talk about something that you have done that was not 'too smart'. Or, talk about a funny occasion that occurred while you were on vacation. Ask others how their day is going. Ask about the

HUMOR

ENJOY LIFE

YOU ONLY HAVE ONE

OPENNESS

WHAT'S YOUR BLUE CHIP

I'LL TELL YOU IF YOU TELL ME

TRUST

CAN I TRUST YOU

DO YOU TRUST ME

REALLY

HUMILITY

BE HUMBLE - EVERYONE SEES YOUR FAULTS ANYWAY

kids, spouse, or their car. Just show that you care about the people around you. We had one manager on our team who was far too intense most of the time. I learned that I could get him to lighten-up at work by asking him about his car. He just loved to talk about his BMW.

Of course there is a time to be serious. If you are dealing with issues, or failings, etc., it's best to be serious. However, overall, make sure that people perceive you as someone who is balanced and who enjoys life. Yes, let's be sure to enjoy life!

OPENNESS

Let's move on to openness. If you are perceived as open, people are more likely to share with you about the challenges *they* are fighting on the job. You will learn about the *real* status of their project; the good and the bad results. Most important, people may even share with you what you could improve or change, about yourself. When people help you improve yourself, you have really struck gold. None of us are perfect. So, it's always useful to collect input about how *I* can improve. Remember that most people will not tell you what they are really thinking about you (they are avoiding conflict), but it's worth asking them anyway. The best way to demonstrate openness is to ask for feedback, and to accept the offered feedback graciously. When people experience your willingness to listen to feedback, they will become open to feedback as well. You must set the proper example. In fact, be sure to be conscious of how you listen. Don't be rehearsing your response to criticism, while you are trying to listen. People can tell if you are listening to their thoughts or not. Really pay attention to what people are trying to tell you.

Many years ago at a management offsite I learned about the 'blue chip'. The idea was to identify one thing about myself that, if I improved, would make a large difference in my results on the job. This item could be a weakness to be improved, but it was often a strength that I possessed that I could further strengthen. That was my 'blue chip' or most valuable item to work on for personal improvement. (In a casino the blue poker chip is the most valuable chip in the house.) I would carry a blue poker chip in my pocket for sixty days to remind myself of what I was striving to improve right now. I would also ask other people to help me with my 'blue chip'. People often felt at ease with this process, and they would ask me what my 'blue chip' was at that time. I could ask them the same question. There was a lot of openness around the topic of 'blue chips'. It became very exciting to be able to have friendly discussions aimed at self-improvement for myself, as well as others. This technique really opened up helpful conversations between managers and their staffs. A great deal of the normal defensiveness during employee performance appraisals just seemed to disappear.

Everyone realized that appraisals were designed to help us all improve the company's results, through self-improvement.

Here's another tough challenge: be open with your boss. Ask your boss for feedback and then quietly listen; don't argue with the feedback. Write down their thoughts, and then go home and think about what you heard. The next time you meet you can ask questions, and if necessary, have some debate. It's always best to know what your boss is thinking about you. If they don't tell you what they are thinking, because you are not open to the feedback, your boss will still be thinking those thoughts about you! It really is best to know what your boss is thinking even if you don't like what you may hear.

TRUST

Let's move on to trust. This character trait is crucial to the operation of a democracy. Free trade requires that people in business are able to trust one another. For example if I purchase a home through a bank mortgage, the bank is trusting that I will make the payments as promised by my signature. And I am trusting that the bank will provide the purchase funds as specified in the mortgage. If either party in this transaction lies and fails to fulfill their commitments, then there will be no profit for either party.

Trust in the workplace is also a two-way street. First, we managers should trust people in general.

We work with many people whom we don't really know very well, and we should initially trust them. We need to give people the benefit of the doubt, unless, there is concrete evidence that they are not trust worthy. For our own mental health, it's best to be a trusting person. Suspicion can drain a lot of your energy, and other people don't like it at all. If someone doesn't deserve your trust, concrete evidence will come to light surprisingly quickly. At that point my advice is to confront the person with this trust issue in a professional way. It is very difficult to work with someone whom you don't trust. It's better for one of you to find another job. I know that that's not always practical. In such cases you will have to keep your eyes open, but it's still best to discuss the trust issues with the other person as they arise. There's always hope that your teammate will change their behavior.

Secondly, we managers should be trust worthy our selves. People in our lives should know that they can believe us. I'm amazed at the number of high profile people who wind up in a divorce, after they have cheated on their spouse. These people then expect to be effective, and trusted in their careers. Personally I believe that if someone has habitually lied to their spouse, then they will most likely lie to their work associates as well. If you follow the guidelines in Chapter One concerning integrity, then trust worthiness is the result in all of your relationships. Integrity is simply being honest with everybody, including your spouse and work associates.

Trust also includes being open and honest about what *I* don't know. If you want people to trust you, don't try to fool them into thinking that you are knowledgeable in a certain arena. You can sadly mislead someone to a false conclusion, with poor results for your entire team. For example if I am naïve about some technical arena that's important to my job, I should be open about that reality. Yes, tell your boss and co-workers that that's the way it is. Then it will be possible for your team to compensate for your short coming, and raise the chances for your team's success. If you hide your naiveté, it could lead to failure for everyone.

It's fairly common in meetings for everyone to act like they 'know it all'. I've been shocked to discover that many people in a meeting do not understand some topic under discussion, when finally one person has the courage to ask for an explanation and admit their ignorance. Many other people in that meeting had the same lack of understanding, but they were willing to fake their knowledge to avoid admitting the truth. They were trying to make themselves look 'good'. It's best to go ahead and ask a question that may sound dumb. If you are willing to admit what you don't know, then people can trust you about what you claim to actually know. I'll discuss this topic more a bit later.

Chapter Three

Be Aggressive - Take Smart Risks

KEY POINT: Be intelligently aggressive in everything you do; remember that without risk there is usually little to gain.

This is the first and probably the most important management principle; and, it's also one of the most difficult principles to master. It's very common for a manager to be either too aggressive, and take too much risk in setting goals, or to be not aggressive enough and take too little risk. It requires a great deal of solid thinking to find the proper balance in your decisions. A manager who is aggressive must also be steadfast, not being too quick to change directions; but a wise manager must know when it is time to stop and change direction. Steadfastness is a virtue, but stubbornness can lead to a disaster. These challenges can sound like a contradiction, but I'd rather call it a paradox.

[By the way I've had several people tell me that they don't like my use of the word 'aggressive'. The connotation can include a personally offensive aspect to the actions of an *aggressive* person. Possibly a better choice of my wording would be the word 'assertive'. However while I do not condone any offensive personal action on someone's part, I prefer the aggressive nature of the word 'aggressive'.]

As you contemplate a business decision be very aware of your self-talk. You need to consider if you are naturally too aggressive, or possibly too risk adverse. Each of us has an inner voice that can emotionally impact our thinking. The challenge is to balance your enthusiasm with your risk aversion. You need to calibrate yourself on this balance. A few people in my experience, get carried away with their enthusiasm. They may fall in love with their idea or invention, and miss the reality of the business situation. They will pursue their idea to their own detriment. Yes, it's important to be tough and steadfast as we face challenges, but don't become blind to likely future failure. Don't let your aggressive self-talk deceive you optimistically about the future.

I believe, however, that most people are actually risk adverse and lack enough enthusiasm. Most people's self-talk is to fear failure, and they consequently procrastinate and don't even get started with their dream. Or, they throttle their own aggressiveness because they fear failure, and don't really get fully committed to their own success. You must plan for success; envision exactly what success will look like in detail. Consciously manage your self-talk to arrive at rational, wise decisions. There must be a balance, but I'd suggest that you error on the side of being more enthusiastic. Leaders actually set the pace for their organization. Go ahead and be aggressive!

BE AT THE RIGHT PLACE

The most important thing to know about being aggressive is to be at the right place at the right time. And, if you determine that you are not, change course sooner rather than later! That is what being aggressive is all about and it's under your control. For example, let's say that you and your company are working on a new AM/FM radio that will be produced very inexpensively. Well if it was the 1940's then this new product could become a business success. However, since it's 2010, you would be better off to just forget about the radio. Either your company needs to change, or you need to find a new company. You may be thinking, "well that's an easy example of an aggressive decision". The point is really rather simple; too many companies pursue products and services that just can't succeed when they are launched into tomorrow's marketplace. Always keep in mind that your product currently under development, must compete not just against current competitors, but also in the future against your competitor's new products. The battle ground is actually in tomorrow's market place. The competitive issue may be cost, features, or just a lack of customers willing to pay your price. You may be working yourself into exhaustion, but you will fail anyway. My product rule of thumb is that if it isn't obviously going to sell *very well* when it's introduced, then stop what you're doing now. You are being aggressive if you stop quickly; or better yet, just don't start that endeavor. Look for a better option. Only take smart risks.

Similarly, if your current job within your company is at a dead end and you find that you are becoming disillusioned, it's best to deal with that reality quickly. Look for another position that has a brighter future, and request a transfer. My experience as a manager is that if you have been doing an excellent job, and you approach your boss for a transfer, then he/she will do whatever they can to meet your needs quickly. Or maybe your skills are a better match to a job in another department; if so, request a transfer. It's always best to aggressively manage your career. Pursue a job which will allow you to succeed and dream of a better future.

I've often wondered why people will often get stuck in their current business activity well after it's become obvious that they are not in the right place at the right time. I believe that we can get stuck, because in order to change the situation, I must recognize that I was wrong when I earlier decided to put myself into this situation. I actually have to face the reality that I made a mistake! Because of our pride this can be psychologically very difficult to do in a timely fashion. The decision to make a change can become very emotionally entangled in our mind. But one of the keys to success is to quickly learn from our mistakes. This may be one of the biggest challenges that you will face as a leader.

A classic example of this psychology is in owning stock on Wall Street. It's relatively easy to decide to buy a particular stock, but very difficult to decide to sell a stock when you are losing money, as it declines in value. We are very inclined to hope that the stock price will rebound positively next week. We want to believe that we made a smart decision to buy the stock in the first place. But, before we can emotionally make the proper decision to sell the stock, the stock price may have dropped fifty percent or more. The answer to this debacle is to aggressively deal with our own emotions. We must become conscious of our self-talk concerning pride. It's best to predetermine quantified decision triggers. The trigger in the stock market example is possibly a ten percent loss in the value of the stock. A possible trigger to abandon a new product under development could be a twenty percent cost increase, or a six month delay in the product's schedule. The best way to deal with our emotions is to set these triggers at the beginning of the project. And of course, be sure to document each trigger in detail, so as to avoid rationalizations when the time for a decision has arrived.

DIFFICULT CONVERSATIONS

Another aspect of being an aggressive leader is to have direct and open conversations with everyone. When speaking with fellow workers be aggressive and get to the point. Certainly don't avoid the point because you are concerned about someone's feelings, or you may be concerned about your own feelings. Don't let negative self-talk dissuade you from saying what needs to be said clearly. You need to be tough, and you need to do it with empathy for the people on your team. Get to the point in a professional manner. You can do that without unnecessarily hurting anyone's feelings. A few years ago I read a great book on this subject, "Difficult Conversations".[5] I highly recommend that you read this book with all of your teammates.

I believe that managers will often avoid direct conversations because they simply don't want to 'face' the other person. Avoiding the issue will just prolong the pain for you, and for the other person. Whenever possible just answer "yes" or "no" to questions, and then explain your thought process. Very often politicians will avoid giving any clear answers when they are interviewed. I guess it takes practice to say nothing and try to sound intelligent. But for a real leader it's best to give clear answers to team members' questions. Managing isn't a popularity contest. You will not be popular for very long if your company is a failure because of you.

Another topic closely related to difficult conversations is conducting too many meetings. You must be ready to say "no" to useless meeting proposals. Be aggressive and conduct only a few, short and pointed meetings. Be clear in writing about why you are calling for a meeting, and be clear about what you will discuss at the meeting. People who are invited to the meeting should do their homework, and be well prepared for the stated topics. If folks are doing their email in your meeting, then you did something wrong either before the meeting or during the meeting. Restructure your meeting plans and make sure that everyone is really engaged in the topic. You may want to reconsider who is invited to the meeting if they are not participating effectively. It would be best to engage in a difficult conversation, and ask them why they are not participating in the meeting.

When the purpose of the meeting is fulfilled, end the meeting. Productivity does matter in successful companies. Be sure to publish the results of your meeting, clearly documenting the decisions and action plans. That way people who were not invited to the meeting for productivity purposes can still be informed about the results of the meeting. Also be sure to follow up on all of the action items from the meeting. Send out emails to all of the people involved with the topic to document the progress of these action items. Be aggressive and hold people accountable to get these action items completed on time. By the way, if someone invites you to a useless meeting, try to help them either redefine the purpose of the meeting, or, just help them cancel the meeting as soon as is possible.

Another particular difficult conversation that people prefer to avoid is negotiations. People will often avoid negotiations because they fear that the discussion will become an emotional conflict. The result of negotiation avoidance is usually measured in paying a high price, in one form or another. This price may be dollar based or it could the loss of emotional satisfaction with a friend. The best way to approach any negotiation is with a plan. When you plan this difficult conversation, you will minimize your fear and maximize your success. Identify the outcome that you would prefer and identify how the other person can meet your desired outcome. Also put yourself in the other person's position. What do you believe is their desired outcome? Usually you can determine a method to allow both of you to be successful. If the situation truly does not allow mutual success, you should understand your negotiation leverage as early as possible. You should strategically establish a plan that will allow you to succeed. But even in this situation try to allow for the other person's desired outcome to the greatest extent possible. In negotiations you should aggressively plan for success, but keep in mind that good will toward the other person is the best attitude.

BE AGGRESSIVE

BE AT THE RIGHT PLACE AT THE RIGHT TIME

####

DIFFICULT CONVERSATIONS ARE VERY GOOD

####

DEMOLISH ROADBLOCKS

####

HIRE THE BEST PEOPLE

####

PUSH TECHNOLOGY - BUT ONLY SO FAR

####

KNOW WHAT YOU DON'T KNOW

DEMOLISH ROADBLOCKS

The next aspect of being an aggressive manager is to not let roadblocks stop your progress. In fact you should expect roadblocks on a daily basis, and you should expect to resolve them quickly. Have a positive attitude in the midst of resolving the roadblock. When you encounter a roadblock analyze the situation, resolve the issue, and move on to the next challenge.

But, periodically be sure to ask yourself if your current endeavor is *still* highly likely to be very successful. Ask yourself if it still obvious that you are working on a winning product. It is possible that one of these roadblocks is a big red warning sign about failure. But after that gut check, if the roadblock is not a red warning sign, push through to the next roadblock, and the next, etc. Success does require a great deal of determination!

HIRE THE BEST

The next thing about being an aggressive manager is to hire the best person for each job. If you have to pay a little extra to hire the best person, do it. It will be worth the premium over the duration of the project. Many studies have indicated that the best person out performs the average person by more than three times in terms of overall results.[6] In addition my experience indicates that the best people will hire the best people. As a result, the improvement in overall results will be multiplied many times over by these 'best' employees. And of course I've seen mediocre performers on the job hire other mediocre performers. My suspicion is that the mediocre hiring manager is intimidated by the best candidate. But if you do hire someone who eventually takes your job, that's real success. An aggressive manager is always looking for their own replacement. Finally when you do hire the best person, be sure to empower them for success. And be sure to take their advice. Yes, ask them for their input on a regular basis.

TECHNOLOGY

If you are working in a high technology organization, as an aggressive manager be sure to push the critical technologies to your advantage. Technology can be your friend if you actively manage it well. For a given time period you can count on certain technologies to improve at a certain rate. For example transistor size in an integrated circuit (Moore's Law) has and will continue to shrink for the next several years. You have to plan for that effect, and even exploit it in your product. Similarly cost effective digital communication band width will continue to improve over the next several years.

However, if you and your company are attempting to create a new technology, or a technology improvement discontinuity from the norm, be very careful. It's easy to convince yourself that this discontinuity will happen quickly, but often the time to market reality is much, much longer than most people antic-ipate. The current example of this foolish aggres-sive thinking is with solar power's impact on the generation of electricity; compared to oil, coal, or natural gas. The local newspapers would lead you to believe that solar power can supply most of our nation's electricity now or next year. The reality is that solar power represents only one to two percent of our electrical consumption today. It will likely take decades before solar power can substantially replace electricity produced by oil across our nation. So yes be aggressive about technology, but don't be foolish. This is often a very difficult decision to make in any business.

KNOW WHAT YOU DON'T KNOW

As an aggressive manager, it is critical that you know what you don't know. We often can inno-cently delude ourselves into thinking that we are smarter than we are in reality. I think this is part of the natural human issue of pride. So, actually sit down and think about this topic! In fact sit down with your whole team and document what you don't know, that may be important to your success.

The Columbia space shuttle disaster is one case to prove this point. The space shuttle had been damaged at lift-off by foam that broke away from the fuel tank. While the shuttle was still in orbit NASA held meetings to discuss the extent of the damage.[7] One very influential engineering manager in the meetings encouraged the executives that the foam could probably not have caused significant damage to the shuttle. Unfortunately he was not an expert in the area of high velocity material ballistics with these particular materials. He did not know what he didn't know. As a result of this engineer's opinion (and several other opinions), the shuttle was not inspected in outer space, and it disintegrated when they attempted reentry into earth's atmosphere. Later ballistic tests proved that it was possible to create very significant damage to the shuttle wing with a high velocity impact of foam.

After you have documented what you don't know that is critical to your success, then you can endeavor to learn about those topics. You may find it necessary to hire someone who is an expert in one or more of these topics. Some topics require years of experience to become an expert, and you may not have the time to try and learn the subject with the necessary depth of knowledge.

Often at work I was fond of admonishing people that "if you don't know what you don't know, you are *dangerous*". This can apply to products, technology, competitors, management processes, financial procedures, etc. How you think about a particular subject depends upon the information in your brain. Be sure that your data base is up to date. You should always be scanning your environment for new information that is relevant to your work. When you are in a meeting be careful how you express your opinion on a subject. There are topics, of course, in which you are an expert. On these topics you can act in a confident manner. But, if you have an opinion on a topic in which you are not an expert, please be careful to inform the meeting attendees that you may be wrong. A little humility is very appropriate in those situations. Right now, start making a list of what you don't know that is relevant to your work. It really is best if you are not dangerous. Your success depends upon it!

Chapter Four

Keep It Simple -
As Simple As Possible

KEY POINT: Always keep your products and your organization as simple as possible; it really does make *life* easier to live.

I love simplicity! Simplicity just makes everything easier. I believe it was Einstein who said something like: a wise person can explain the complicated, in a simple fashion. In my own experience I've found that when someone really understands something, they can explain it to me quickly and in a simple manner. It does take a great deal of understanding and insight to communicate the essence of a given topic. When I was in college, the subject of Physics always appealed to me. It's amazing to be able to understand the essential basics of what makes something work the way it does (or to understand *why* something does not work.) But there are topics that, by there nature, are complicated. For example the organization chart of a one thousand person company is not simple. However, don't make it more complicated than necessary. I've seen organization structures that are hopelessly contorted on paper, and in reality. No one could understand how the company actually got work done, including the employees.

ORGANIZATION STRUCTURE

The first topic that's best kept simple is organization structures. An organization should be lean and to the point. It's always best to maximize management ratios. This enables quicker decisions, and keeps the expense costs lower. It's far too easy to erroneously grow an organization with too many managers. For example, employees will often push for promotions, and it's easy to quickly approve their request. Resist this inclination to say "yes", in order to maximize your efficiency. I always tried to keep a manager's span of control to a minimum of five direct reports with a maximum of ten direct reports. These numbers enable great productivity.

Also, design the organization so that responsibility and authority are as clear as possible. Try to assign the organizational names to be self-descriptive of what each organization actually does every day. Minimize any overlap in responsibilities.

Feuding can often result if two people believe that they are both responsible for a particular decision. Each group's responsibility should be as obvious as possible, and when it's not obvious be sure to document everyone's authority and responsibility. Ask your team for suggestions on how to streamline work flows. Always strive to be the champion of simplicity.

When possible try to under staff projects somewhat. Fewer people will translate into less communication overhead and less confusion. The frequent problem is that many managers will argue for additional people in their group, hoping to earn themselves a raise or a promotion. Unfortunately management pay scales are often linked to the department manager's expense or head count. As a great leader in search of simplicity you will need to say "no" at the proper time. Be mindful that it always seems easier to hire people today, than it is to reduce the number of people in the future.

PRODUCTS AND SERVICES

Products should also be kept as simple as possible. Feature creep can be the enemy of low cost and time to market. During the product definition and development stage as features are added to a product, it's very difficult to track the product's total cost. Usually at the end of multiple discussions which repeatedly added features to the product, everyone is negatively surprised when the costs are accurately reported to the team weeks later. Then it takes even more time to agree to remove features in an intelligent manner through even more meetings. In addition everyone must realize that the product development elapsed time increases substantially as more features are included in the development phase of the product. All of this feature creep further delays the introduction of the product and then delays the revenue that was expected from the product shipments. The bottom line on adding too many features to a new product is really bad news, period.

Of course, the best approach to product definition is to know your potential customers. You should have a clear idea of 'why' these customers will buy your product or service. You should also clearly know how much these customers are willing to pay for your product or service. The benefits and cost for your customers should be well understood. In addition you should have a solid understanding of your future competition. Your product must exceed your customer's expectations, as set by their real needs, and be mindful of the competitor's product offering. Be sure to exceed your customer's expectations but not by too much margin. Keep in mind that too many added features will raise your costs and delay the product's introduction into the market. If your competitors over shoot the customer's needs, you don't necessarily have to follow them and make the same mistake. You can offer your product at a lower price. But, if you set your price too low you are probably making a different mistake, and leaving profits behind. It's always exciting to dominate a market with the lowest price, but you should make sure you understand the associated impact to your business. Sometimes it's smarter to aim for a sixty percent market share and be the number one player in the market, versus trying to garner an eighty percent market share and totally dominate the market. If you are sacrificing a high gross margin for that market domination, it's probably best to rethink your pricing strategy. Wall Street will reward you for keeping your gross margin respectably high.

Keep in mind that after you have introduced your product into the market it's always possible to launch a more expensive, more featured product at a later date. Apple Inc. is an absolute expert at utilizing this strategy, for example, with the IPoD product family. This strategy has allowed them to defend themselves against low cost competition while adding sophisticated features over time, to actually raise the customer's expectations. Their competition has not been able to execute effectively against this strategy. You must be careful, however, about adding features to a product. I've often been amazed that customers may prefer a simpler product that offers better ease of use characteristics. Once again, Apple is masterful at providing sophisticated features, and, providing excellent ease of use. But do be very careful; if you try to serve too many

KEEP 'IT' SIMPLE

KISS

####

KEEP 'IT' SIMPLE PLEASE; AT LEAST AS SIMPLE AS POSSIBLE

####

'IT' INCLUDES ORGANIZATIONS, PRODUCTS, TECHNOLOGY, AND LIFE

diverse needs with a single product, that can often lead to serving *no* market very well.

TECHNOLOGY

Most of all, your company's use of technology should be kept as simple as is possible. This approach to the use of technology will give you a much higher probability of success. There's no point in taking additional risk if you can accomplish your business goals with a technology that is well understood. I believe that many start-up companies in Silicon Valley fail because the founders under-estimated the technical challenges that they were undertaking with their product plans. In many cases it was not necessary to be so aggressive with the technology, but engineer's egos can often push them to the 'bleeding edge' (beyond the 'cutting edge') of technology, for bragging rights at dinner meetings. In today's semiconductor technology it's possible to implement very complex circuits with 90 nanometer design rules. These circuits are relatively easy to design in that technology and the manufacturing costs are very low. However many new companies are, instead, trying to design their products with 32 nanometer design rules, even though they could bring their product to market with less aggressive design rules. It's always best to minimize the technical risks in order to maximize your probability of success.

If it really is necessary to be dramatically aggressive with technology, be sure that you and your team are experts in that technology. Make sure that you know what you don't know! And, be sure to add time into your product schedules for the unexpected problems that are sure to arise during development. It's never easy to be one of the early users of any technology. I would encourage you to properly estimate the risks before proceeding on the 'bleeding edge' of technology. If you do succeed on the 'bleeding edge' you will have earned those associated bragging rights over dinner. But if you fail because you underestimated the complexity of the technology, you will feel very disappointed with yourself, and you may have consumed a great deal of money in the process. In the early stages of your companies' existence, maybe, you should consider some other less risky business venture that would be better to pursue with your resources and with your time. Once your business is launched and you are spending money, it's very difficult psychologically to stop or change what you are doing despite the mounting evidence of underestimated risk. We humans find it very difficult to admit when we are wrong.

OVERALL OBJECTIVES

Finally as you pursue your dream of success, if your business endeavor becomes more and more complicated, don't start counting on too many 'miracles' occurring in order for your business and career to succeed. Keep it simple, stupid, could be the best advice you have ever heard. Business is tough enough without trying to accomplish the seemingly impossible. A key question to periodically ask your self is: has my dream become far too complicated and unlikely to succeed? If the answer is "no", proceed with assurance. If the answer is "yes", only proceed after you have completed a thorough inventory of all of the breakthroughs that are necessary to assure success. In order to maximize the probability of success, analyze the work to determine if you can further simplify your endeavor. If you find that you need only one major breakthrough, success is possible but not highly probable. If you require two or more breakthroughs, stop what you are doing now. You must find a way to simplify what you are attempting to accomplish. It may be useful to read the discussion about taking too much risk in Chapter 3 again. There may be a better alternative place for you to be in business at this point in time. It's wonderfully exhilarating to be aggressive, but it's also very easy to get carried away with your dreams.

LIFE

I can't help adding that simplicity is also wonderful in your daily life. The world has become enamored with acquiring money and things, but little do we realize how this effort complicates living. Everything we own requires time and maintenance; soon we become slaves to our possessions. We need to constantly ask ourselves how we can attain true satisfaction in life. Once you answer that question, then you can know that everything else will become a distraction, without satisfaction. Even in our daily life we should know that simplicity will give us the best opportunity to fulfill our dreams.

Chapter Five

Focus - And Focus Again

KEY POINT: Focus is crucial to getting things done quickly and successfully; it's often necessary to say "no" to a myriad of distractions.

To be successful you must be productive. It's necessary that on a daily basis you and your team must accomplish predefined goals. The only way to get things done is to be focused. Focus is achieved by saying "no" at the right time. That sounds strange, but I believe it's true. If you are busy getting your work completed, and someone interrupts you with a college basketball score, it's very enticing to check out the last play on the internet. Or more seriously, if you are busy developing a product for one market, and someone brings you an interesting new idea for another market, what do you need to do at that juncture? Yes, you have to say "no" with a positive attitude. You have to remain focused on the task at hand, until it is completed. Of course you also want to be polite and get back to that person and their new idea, at the right time. I always keep a 'parking lot' of new ideas that may be worth pursuing at some future date, after I'm finished with the current work. The current work was most likely, also, a new idea from the past. Just write down the new idea in your 'parking lot', on a piece of paper or in a computer file. Assure this person with the new idea that you will revisit the idea at the right time in the future.

Going one step further it would be most productive to build an office environment which inherently limits your interruptions. When you are involved in deep thinking, put up a sign at the door of your cubical that says: "Please do NOT interrupt". Also have a method to turn off your phone during these time periods. Keep in mind that if you are interrupted once in an hour for only five minutes, and it requires several minutes to reinitiate your thought pattern, you have lost fifteen percent of your productivity! In fact a recent study of software engineers found that they only spend an average of eleven minutes on one task before they are interrupted to deal with another activity.[8] That is a loss of productivity in excess of fifty percent. Interruptions can certainly be very expensive.

JUST SAY "NO"

So, this chapter is all about learning to say "no". Now doesn't that sound nice and simple? But, it's not easy to do for the typical human being. Life is full of distractions and enticements; as a result, we have to *learn* to say "no". I believe that this is a learned skill.

The difference between a child and a mature adult is often in the ability to focus on what is really important and ignore everything else. So be an adult. OK, I'm trying to motivate you by implied insult! But, each of us must learn to live our daily lives with discipline. In a leadership role, focus can really be difficult because we are surrounded by very smart employees who believe that, in addition to what we are now doing on the job, more things can and should be done as well. We are always going to be asked to do more. Smart people including you have many, many good ideas. But successful leaders pick out the best ideas, and then stay focused long enough to be successful. Focus means sticking with the most important tasks; no jumping around is allowed until success is secure. Discipline really does matter in business and in life.

CLEAR GOALS

The best way to successfully say "no" to distractions is to know what to say "yes" to each day. Each person in an organization should have documented clear goals for this year, quarter, week, and today. The annual goals should be comprised of no more than ten items, with the top three clearly identified for emphasis. These goals should be as quantified as possible so that at the end of the year they can be measured by you and your manager. The quarterly and weekly goals should be limited to at most three items, of course based upon the annual goals. The goals for today should be limited to one or two items. First thing in the morning I always try to write down what my focus is for today. Write down that one item that will get done today, for sure! I take that piece of paper and stick it in my pocket as a constant reminder to keep me focused. You can also put that one item into your lap top or PDA screen saver as your reminder. Then as the day unfolds and I'm distracted by some urgent interruption, the piece of paper reminds me to quickly get back to my focus item. Day after day it requires a constant vigilance to stay focused and be successful.

It's also very important to keep the key annual and quarterly organizational goals visible to all of the employees. Bumper stickers can be very useful as 'sticky' reminders for employees. Use any technique necessary to help keep yourself and others properly focused on the key goals. These techniques could include posters, web pages, emails, or even bumper stickers. It's very useful to boil down a key goal to a few words, so it's easy to remember and it fits on a bumper sticker. If you can't capture a key goal in a few words, maybe you need to really think about the essence of that goal. Or, it's possible that you need to identify a better, simpler key goal that will lead you to success. A simple description is the best way to insure that the entire team fully understands what is being achieved through their work. I'm sure you know the old story of the two stone cutters. One was highly motivated because he was working on a cathedral. The other was bored and listless because he was cutting, yet, another stone without the cathedral in his 'mind's eye'. The proper definition of organizational goals, and linked personal goals, can lead to highly motivated focused people.

BE SPECIAL

A funny thing happens as you sharpen your focus; you become special. You can become the best at whatever you do, if you focus your energy on your specialty. So if what you do is valuable in the world's marketplace (be at the right place at the right time), and you are the best at what you do; then, you have a great chance of being successful. This can apply to an individual or to an entire company. Success is all about specialization which leads to excellence. Most people think that it's valuable to be a 'jack of all trades'. But in most cases that's just not true. Most people can't excel in many talents simultaneously. Many people get a false sense of security by attempting to be a 'jack of all trades'. These folks believe that if they get laid off by their current employer, then they will more easily be able to find another job with their broad skills. However it would be best for them to focus on retaining their current job by being an expert, rather than planning for a potential release from their current job. In this modern world it's usually the experts who are retained, promoted, and highly paid. So for yourself and for your company, pick a focus and become an expert. If in the course of time it turns out that your specialization is no longer in demand, then plan to switch to a new specialty. The switch will take some time so be sure to anticipate this requirement by a year or two. This approach to specialization will give you the highest probability of success in your career.

PRIORITIZE RESOURCES

The need for focus includes your time and energy, and, it also includes your resources. If you are employed as a manager I'm sure that the resources at your disposal far exceed the value of your own personal time. These resources include all the people that you influence, plus money, equipment, etc. Are you managing all of these resources in a manner consistent with your key goals? Can you *specifically* answer this crucial question? There's only one way to really be able to give an appropriate answer: are

FOCUS

FOCUS BY SAYING "NO" WITH A POSITIVE ATTITUDE

####

WHAT'S YOUR GOAL TODAY

####

BUMPER STICKERS STICK

####

SPECIALIZE UNTIL YOUR SPECIAL

####

PRIORITIZE RESOURCES

you measuring the effectiveness of your resource deployment? You have to check and verify through measurement techniques, that your resources are deployed where you really want them to be utilized each day. For example effective generals know where their troops are today and where they will be tomorrow. Battles are fought and won through focused resource deployment. I often found it to be a useful exercise to look at the size of each of my organizations, and check that they were scaled to our business priorities. It's easy to have one group of people grow too quickly, through rapid hiring, while another group grows slowly through careful hiring; only picking the few outstanding candidates that they were able to interview. It's up to you as the responsible manager to keep your organizations in proper balance.

Of course it's also important to verify that the resources the company has entrusted to you are actually achieving the proper goals. I often found it useful to ask other employees, especially my direct reporting managers, what their top goal was for this current week. As I was walking into our cafeteria, it was always a great conversation starter to simply ask someone about their top priority. By doing this in a friendly way you convey that you care about that person, and you care about the company as well. Effective generals need to visit the front lines periodically, and ask the troops about their activities. At HP this practice was commonly referred to as management by walking around. These conversations can then easily move into a discussion of the progress that is being achieved toward your goals. Hopefully everything is proceeding according to the established plan. If not it's very gratifying to ask if you can help in some way; the person will feel very encouraged and may even accept your offer for assistance.

All too often during these conversations with 'the troops', I would discover that people did not perceive the same priorities that I had assumed were agreed to by the management team. At that point I found that it was best to jot down a note to myself, and I would speak to that person's manager later in private, in order to resolve the situation. Sometimes it was a simple misunderstanding, but more often I found that the manager and I did not really agree on the goals. I had been *assuming* that there was agreement across the entire team. This was an opportunity to make sure that our resources had been properly prioritized across the organization.

Another prioritization technique that worked very well was our 'all employee' quarterly update meeting. I would simply spend one hour with various groups of people to discuss our key projects results from the past quarter and the key goals for the new quarter. This was a superb method to ensure that everyone across the organization had a clear direction. After every one of these meetings at least one person would chat with me about the presentation, because they thought there were different priorities. This is a wonderful way to clear the air and resolve the different opinions that will certainly exist within any group of people.

Chapter Six

Measure It - or Don't Do It

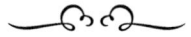

KEY POINT: In business and in life set goals that can be measured, so you can know for sure that you are making progress.

In a business environment if there's something worth doing, then it should be critical to the results that you expect from your endeavor. And if it is a critical activity, then you had better know how you will verify progress toward these results during that activity. Of course in management, the classic bad example is a project that will require many years to complete, and no one is effectively checking on valid intermediate milestones. When the project winds up a year late with poor quality, and way over budget, everyone seems surprised by the negative results. But the sloppy management team actually got the results they should have anticipated at the start of this project. Any well managed activity should include a detailed status report on a monthly basis. Meaningful intermediate milestones should be defined at the beginning of a project. Then, as the project proceeds, there should be red flags raised by the team if these intermediate milestones are running behind schedule.

I've also noticed that managers who don't set well defined goals will usually not appropriately delegate responsibility and authority. They fear that they will not really be able to track the progress of the project unless they retain the authority for themselves. This leads to micromanagement and frustration for everyone. This is a very ineffective way to manage an organization.

START RIGHT

I believe that the key to organizing a successful project is at the start of the various activities. Experienced people know that getting started in an organized fashion will lead to the appropriate management discipline over the length of the project. When you start an activity in an undisciplined manner, psychologically it's very difficult to later stop and put the proper methodology in place. As I discussed before people do not like to admit that they made a mistake and change direction. That's why when serious troubles arise on a project, it's usually necessary to hire or transfer a new manager into the project to change to the proper methodology.

At the beginning of a project the team should document the key goals in a manner that permits direct, easy measurement of those goals. The document should be placed under change control by the senior management. During the course of the project before any goal is modified, key players in the team should be required to approve the change in writing. As changes occur in the project it's also useful to check that the resulting product or service will still be a great success, as originally intended by the company. For example, it's not unusual during a long project for a product's cost to increase, and it's possible that the product is no longer going to be competitive. It's mandatory that product costs are tracked in detail as the project proceeds toward completion.

REAL STATUS REVIEWS

Once the project is launched monthly status reviews should be conducted with key team members in attendance. Progress reports should be presented with clarity, including a great amount of measurable, factual data. These meetings must be held with an open and honest attitude; everyone must be 'real'. If the project is on schedule then there is reason for celebration. But if schedules are being missed for some reason, then these facts must be discussed with recovery plans agreed to by the team. Tough and intelligent questions must be encouraged, and directly answered before proceeding to other topics. All too often these types of meetings become a feel good show, and people become defensive when tough questions are raised by anyone. If this atmosphere becomes prevalent the project is doomed at that point. When negative facts are being hidden or avoided, it becomes impossible to identify a recovery plan. As a leader one of your responsibilities is to encourage everyone to be open and honest, especially with negative results or information. One of the best ways to encourage openness is to set the correct example. Always remember that people are watching how you handle tough questions or the reporting of negative results. If you react in a defensive emotional manner to poor reported results, people will stop making those reports. The results may continue to be poor in reality, but you will not hear about that reality. Or if your reaction to a tough question is to ignore it, or even worse to disparage the questioner, then people will simply stop asking those appropriate tough questions. Smart managers always want to really know what is going on, at the battle field level. You must encourage an open flow of information.

MEASURE IT - OR DON'T DO IT

INSPECT TO GET WHAT YOU EXPECT

THE PROJECT START IS KEY

WHAT WILL YOU MEASURE

MEASURE TWICE - CUT ONCE

THINK TWICE - ERROR LESS

FIX IT NOW

Always keep in mind that it's best to solve problems as early as possible. If people are trying to hide their problems, thinking that they will resolve the issue before you can discover it, then they are setting things up for failure by possibly postponing the real problem resolution. In an open environment where people trust each other, they quickly look to the team for help. The manager's attitude toward discussing issues will determine how people handle the flow of critical information. The classic case in software projects involves finding and fixing bugs. Software engineers will often avoid reporting bugs in their own code, in order to avoid the necessity to explain 'why' that bug occurred in their code. But by sharing the cause of a bug with peers, it's often possible to find other existing bugs due to the exact same cause. Many engineers also want to avoid peer code reviews for the same reasons. However it costs over one thousand times more to fix a bug reported by a customer, then if the programmers find that same bug in a code review procedure, before the product is shipped to customers. Peers can help find and resolve problems if each team member is willing to accept help from one another.

The bottom line is to manage in a way that will encourage the identification and open discussion of problems. That approach to project management will identify problems early, and allow for a rapid resolution to the problem. The whole purpose of monthly status reviews is to report issues, and then ensure that they are resolved quickly. In addition I've also found it useful to have private one hour meetings every two weeks with each person on my staff. These meetings allowed us to catch up on the project's status, and discuss possible problems before they became acute.

LEARN FROM MISTAKES

Finally, it's possible to gauge the quality of a team by the number of problems they report. For example an excellent team who has many years of experience together, doing similar projects, will report fewer problems. They will simply make fewer mistakes because they have the appropriate experience. They have learned from their past mistakes and they are able to deliver a successful project more efficiently. Each of their projects will demonstrate a learning ability, and growth in effective results. On the other hand if your team is reporting a large number of problems, and doesn't seem to be learning from their mistakes, then you must take action. It may be necessary to take some time out of the project for special intense training. Or it may be necessary to bring into the project some managers with much more experience.

You must be very careful how you react to this particular problem reporting metric. It's very easy for team members to stop reporting problems if they perceive that management is penalizing people for honestly reporting the problems that they encounter. As a manager you must react to poor results, but only in a fashion that is perceived as being fair and effective by the team members. Problems are often the result of someone habitually not properly performing their job. A question I often asked the team is: "who has to change what behavior". But of course when asking the question, it's best to avoid sounding onerous.

In general, inexperienced teams will resist documenting goals, conducting monthly reviews, and reporting problems. People will often view these activities as unnecessary overhead and a waste of time. The reality is that these activities are overhead. But it's your job to convince people that this overhead is absolutely necessary for a successful project, and for efficient learning on the job. If goals are not documented they can be forgotten or misunderstood a few months later. If monthly reviews are not conducted effectively, no one can really know if the project is on schedule. And if problems are not reported, they will most likely not get thoroughly fixed in a rapid fashion. In fact the easiest way to check on the maturity of a team is to watch how whole heartedly they react to setting goals and measuring their monthly results.

QUALITY

Excellence is achieved by building proper team habits! Quality in your product is the result of repeatedly following well defined processes with clear documented goals. Quality is never an accident; it is a habit. The habits of experienced, successful teams include encouraging each other to follow the documented procedures. Short cuts to results very often wind up in a 'ditch'. Just a few years ago I recall acquiring a company that seemingly possessed a new high speed communication technology. The employees had a great deal of university knowledge, but very little actual development experience. They committed to deliver a product with the highest speed in the industry in a very short time frame. To make a very long painful story short, the product never did work in a reliable fashion under varying temperature conditions. We later learned that due to the team's inexperience, their testing procedures were woefully abbreviated in order to fulfill the schedule. I should have monitored their product development practices in much more detail. I should have inspected their procedures in order to get what I expected from that team. Our customers and we suffered with poor quality for several years as a result of this failure.

The Japanese industrial complex dramatically improved their quality over the past fifty years by simply establishing thorough operational habits that led to predictable, high quality results. They also understood that there is a need to innovate and improve these work processes. But they understood that these innovations must also be managed properly as they are newly deployed in a work force. In my experience, unfortunately, I've seen too many American impetuous engineers introducing supposed innovations in a sloppy, ill thought out fashion. The result is usually a significant deterioration of quality which can persist for a surprisingly long period of time. Unintended consequences are always a possibility unless we carefully think through the implications of innovations before they are implemented by a work force. Of course we are all aware that the Japanese approach to quality has given them a clear lead in the automotive market. This management approach that employs careful, consistent measurement of progress towards documented, well established goals often yields the best results over the long term. Because I live and work in Silicon Valley, I often observe the naïve short term mindset that leads to 'one too many' short cuts during the development of a new product. I believe that this is one of the key reasons why so many start-up companies end in failure. If you exercise the principles of Measure It - or Don't Do It, you will be much better off in the long term.

Chapter Seven

A Company Is Only As Good As The People

KEY POINT: Always remember that people are your company's most valuable resource; and that definitely includes you.

At the end of a work day when all of the employees have gone home, what of your company is left behind? Basically there is nothing of real value left. Oh sure there are buildings, equipment, and in some cases intellectual property left behind, but without dedicated people the company is not worth much at all. In fact it required intelligent people to build those buildings, buy that equipment, and design the intellectual property. The bottom line is that a company's most important resource is the people. So doesn't it make sense that this resource should be treated with great care, in terms of nurturing these people and hiring even more, competent people. To emphatically make this point at Xilinx, our Founder and CEO Bernie Vonderschmitt designed an organization chart that put him at the bottom of the sheet, and all of the employees were at the top of the organization. We posted these 'inverted' organization charts in all of the conference rooms to make sure that everyone remembered that *they* were the key to the success of the company. This mindset propelled Xilinx to a $8 billion market capitalization in 2006. But even more impressive Xilinx and our employees were ranked in FORTUNE Magazine's "Ten Best Places To Work" for four consecutive years! As a team we celebrated in our mutual success.

TRAINING

All of the services and products of any company are generated by people. These people require training, motivating, and rewards for great work. Since a company is only as good as the employees, it's a necessary corollary that a company can only improve if the people improve. Each person should be challenged to grow and develop on their job. You should set the example in this area! Ask yourself: "How are you striving to improve?" Do people around you perceive that you are interested in growing *your* skills?

Training is absolutely necessary for everyone. Certainly newly hired people should take classes,

A COMPANY IS ONLY AS GOOD AS THE PEOPLE

A COMPANY CAN ONLY IMPROVE IF THE PEOPLE IMPROVE

####

I MUST IMPROVE

####

HIRE THE BEST PEOPLE

####

PROMOTE THE BEST PEOPLE

but training is much more than just classes. As a manager you should ensure that each employee has an effective mentor. Be sure to select these mentors with great care; their approach to work will become highly influential. And that's exactly the point of assigning mentors; these mentors become the role models in your organization. A mentor can ensure that what a new employee learns from a class will be appropriately applied to every day work situations. The best way to learn is on the job with a great deal of practice. If someone has been on their job for many years, they also need training. Sometimes people can get stale on their job and new ideas simply stop occurring, or, are even resisted by that employee. It's often a very good idea to speak with these folks to find out if it may be a good time for a change in job assignment. Every employee should have a mentor. If someone has been on their job for a long time, the mentor can suggest new approaches to the work. Or the mentor can provide coaching and encourage the person to move into a new position when that's appropriate. Mentors can provide the impetus for growth and development across your whole organization. Training classes in most companies are ineffective, boring, and de-motivating. Other than these *few* problems, training classes are very important! It's most appropriate to put one of your top employees in charge of periodically reviewing classes to ensure that they are effective and motivating. All classes and teachers should receive student grading with suggestions for improvement. Also, be sure that you are setting the proper example when it comes to training. Are you taking classes periodically? Are you working as a mentor to another employee? Do you have a mentor to help you grow on the job?

MOTIVATION

It's also very critical to properly motivate your teammates. In a recent Gallop survey of employees, it was revealed that half of the people were actually not mindfully engaged in their work.[9] Clearly the productivity of our work force is reduced when people are distracted and not motivated to deliver excellent results. A company will be most successful when the employees are thinking about their work; a great company doesn't just employ a body on the job.

I want to emphasize that motivation is primarily about the job, itself. Ask yourself what can you do to ensure that every job in your group is as stimulating as possible to that employee? Please make certain that the job and the employee are well matched to each other. For example a quiet individual may not be the best person to select as a WalMart store greeter. Or in the case of engineers they usually prefer a job that is more open ended in terms of technology. If it's possible even let the employee help you define their job responsibilities.

A COMPANY IS ONLY AS GOOD AS THE PEOPLE

MOTIVATION - IT'S ALL ABOUT THE JOB

####

SMART PEOPLE SOLVE PROBLEMS GENIUSES PREVENT PROBLEMS

####

ALWAYS ASSOCIATE WITH THE BEST PEOPLE

####

ENCOURAGE PEOPLE - IT'S FREE

If the employee is dissatisfied with their job, nothing you do will be effective in building a motivated employee unless you change the job content. Many of our work responsibilities today are actually team responsibilities. Teams of employees may need help to better relate to one another, and to better understand one another's expectations. Team building sessions that are focused on business goal definition and work methods can yield great team output. Personally I believe that the pure team building approach is a waste of time; always tie the team building to your business goals.

Rewarding people for excellent work results is mandatory. Thoroughly investigate salary structures in your industry and make sure that your company's salary structure is competitive. You want to ensure that your people believe that they are being treated fairly, and you also want to ensure that you can recruit excellent new hires when necessary.

Within your salary structure you must ensure that the people who are most responsible for the company's success are rewarded at the highest level. I believe that the employees who contribute the most to success should receive the highest income. This seems obvious to most people, but I've been amazed at the number of times that, after checking, I've found great employees in the middle of the pay scale. There have been many excuses offered to me, but these situations need to be rectified as quickly as possible. However you must be careful about how you determine which employees are contributing the most to success. It's very easy to conclude that a person who is solving many problems has contributed a great deal to the success of a project. But, be sure to check into who is responsible for originating those problems. If it's one and the same person, then they may actually be responsible for delaying the project. Always keep in mind that smart people solve problems, but the best people prevent problems.

It's always most effective to utilize a team approach when determining salaries and raises. Sometimes the direct manager can be biased by a friendship that has developed at work, and as a result, they do not really perceive which employee is the highest contributor. A team of peer managers should be assembled annually to review salaries for their teams. It's critical that all employees believe that they are being fairly evaluated and compensated financially.

I also believe that employees should receive bonuses for contributions beyond the normal call of duty. It's actually not about the amount of money that's granted to the employee, but the real advantage is in the recognition given with the bonus. The recognition can either be given publically or privately. It's about encouraging people when they do well. As a leader one of your key roles is to be an encourager. People just love to go home and share with their spouses about how they were given a special compliment from their manager. Often it's useful to give an employee or an entire team special recognition without any financial bonus. During a team meeting all you need to do is mention by name the person who performed at an exceptional level. Or possibly send out an email that is complimentary of that person. That individual will feel very special and may even remember the occasion for many years. When people feel special they enjoy coming into work each morning. Anything that you can do that reduces the amount of complaining at work will improve overall productivity. When someone spends their time complaining they are not spending their time getting work accomplished. And to make matters worse, they are also wasting the time of another employee who is listening to them complain. This is one of the reasons why layoffs are so damaging to productivity. The people who have not been released from the company will spend months and years complaining about the other people who were mistreated during the layoff, in their humble opinion.

Also be very careful about distributing large executive bonus's which are not clearly linked to business goals. Certainly that type of compensation is not appropriate, just ask your stock holders. In addition most employees will believe that these payouts are unfair, leading to a lot of complaining and wasted time on the job.

When tough times arrive in your industry or in the world as is currently the case, treat employees with as much tender loving care as is possible. For example if the down turn appears to be temporary, it may be best to do pay reductions across the employee base before resorting to layoffs. I can recall about a decade ago at Xilinx, we announced that in order to avoid layoffs we would all receive a pay cut for several quarters. The executives actually received the largest percentage cuts in the company. The amount of good will that was created with the employee base was astounding, and it persisted for many years. People felt that the management team had acted fairly, and they could be trusted to take the right action. All of the employees felt that they were a team who could work together and suffer together, in order to manage through the down turn.

Speaking of layoffs, as I've described it's best to only do them if it is absolutely necessary. A layoff program should not replace proper employee performance management. Every employee should be coached by their manager, and they should be given accurate, timely feedback on their job performance. In addition every employee deserves to receive a documented annual performance appraisal. If the employee is not contributing at minimum expectations for their job, after a period of time with coaching, they should be told that they will be dismissed in thirty days unless a dramatic improvement occurs in their productivity. Most people in that situation will chose to leave the company of their own volition. If they do not leave and they do not improve their work output, then they should be dismissed quickly after the thirty days has elapsed. In my experience it's actually better for that person to find a job through which they can perform well and be successful. We're not doing an employee a favor by letting them remain in a job in which they can't succeed. In addition it's also better for the other employees on that team. Usually people know when a team member is not contributing at the appropriate level, and, they are often struggling to try to compensate for that team member by carrying an additional work load. Very quickly resentment can build and management is blamed for not taking the appropriate action.

In summary proper overall motivation of people is crucial to your success as a leader. When people feel valued by the management team, they not only work harder, but they also work smarter. For example Wim Roelandts, our CEO at Xilinx, would often comment that he had never seen a de-motivated engineer create a great new idea. If you are expecting people to create new and better ideas, the work environment needs to be positive and uplifting.

PROMOTIONS

Promotions of course can be very exciting and encouraging. Promotions are also crucial to the success of your company, so be very careful about how you determine who should be promoted into a particular position. If you have an open position in your organization, write down the necessary qualifications and scan for potential candidates within your organization. In addition speak with the team members about possible candidates. Speak with other managers in your company about additional candidates. Finally at this point you are ready to start the interview process. Interviewers should include you, other managers, and a few of the team members. At the conclusion of the interviews collect all of the feedback and make a reasonably quick selection of a person for the promotion. It's best not to keep everyone in suspense for too long a period of time. But if you can't find an excellent candidate within the company, then proceed to search for candidates with proper qualifications outside the company. You will do a terrible disservice to everyone on this team if you promote a current employee who is not appropriate for the job. The bottom line is that promotions and hiring should be taken very seriously and done *extremely* well.

SOAR WITH EAGLES

Here is one last thought on people: always spend your time on the job with the best people. If you are a great employee, you will surround yourself with other great employees. In hindsight my most exciting years on the job were during the times that

I had the privilege to be part of an awesome team of people. I'd rather soar with eagles than struggle with failure. However, sometimes human fear can cause us to worry that another great employee on the team may someday take my job away from me. Well, that is true; but, that's also the best way to work. You should always be doing succession planning together with your manager. If your fear causes you to shun great people, then, you are not a great employee! In that case it's time for you to improve yourself, and begin looking out for the best interests of your company. I'm quite sure that your manager will notice and appreciate your new attitude.

Chapter Eight

Conclusion

Consistent with my intent to keep this book simple, I'd like to offer a one paragraph conclusion.

Always live and work with integrity; be honest with yourself and all the people whom you impact on a daily basis. Keep in mind that your character is on display at all times. Be intelligently aggressive in everything you do; remember that without risk there is usually little to gain. Always keep your products and organization as simple as is possible; it really does make life easier to live. Focus is crucial to getting things done quickly and successfully; it's often necessary to say "no" to a myriad of distractions. In business and in life set goals that are measurable, so you can know for sure that you are making progress. Finally, always remember, that people are your company's most valuable resource; and, that definitely includes you!

As you practice these ten leadership principles, you will be actively building a culture for your company. It will be a culture of human respect with a focus on delivering effective results. I wish you success.

Appendix

'Success' According To God

I'm a dedicated Christian. Jesus is my number one priority in life. I try to pray and read my Bible on a daily basis. Hence, many of you will likely conclude that I'm emotionally biased when it comes to the topic of God. But I'm not an emotional zealot; I'm logical and intellectual. How did I get to this point in my belief about God? About twenty five years ago I started to intensely analyze and investigate my beliefs about God. I spoke with a lot of people with various opinions, and I began to study the Bible. To make a very long story short, I logically concluded that the Bible had to be inspired by God. God has chosen to tell us about Himself through this book. Many people want to invent their own God, but God anticipated our arrogance and revealed Himself to us. How do I know that I can believe the Bible? After twenty plus years of studying and teaching the Bible, I'm constantly amazed at the wisdom and consistency of this book. The Bible was written by forty plus authors over a period of more than fifteen hundred years, and yet the Bible gives us a consistent description of God. Archaeology has also confirmed a great deal of the content of the Bible. So, based upon my intellectual analysis, I believe the Bible. If you are not sure for yourself, I'd suggest that you read "The Case For Christ", by Lee Strobel.[10] He was a legal investigative reporter in Chicago who did his own extensive investigation to prove to his wife that Christianity was false. He concluded that in a court of law there is more than ample evidence to conclude that the Bible is accurate, and that Jesus is God. His book is a thorough treatment of his investigation and decision to become a dedicated Christian. He is now one of the most popular Christian speakers in America.

My God is Jesus. The Bible actually enables me to know Jesus through His words and actions. He loves me so much that He died on that cross for me and for you. His death was necessary because, for the sake of justice, someone had to pay for my sins of lying, cheating, stealing, etc. Only Jesus, who is God, could pay the price of the sins of billions of human beings. Now that my sins are paid for I have the free gift of heaven, because I have put my faith in Jesus and agreed to follow Him. You can be guaranteed of heaven as well, if you accept His death for your sins and agree to follow Him. If you really want to know Jesus, pray and ask Him to reveal Himself to you. Jesus wants to communicate with you as your God. The Bible clearly tells us that Jesus is God and the Savior of the world. If you want more information please check out www. meant4more.com, and watch the videos about what Jesus has to say in the Bible concerning His love for us.[11] You can also participate in the various chat rooms about the Christian faith.

The Bible also has a lot to say about how we should live and work. There are many great words of wisdom in the Bible! For example in the Bible the book of Proverbs 1:5 (chapter 1 and verse 5) says: "A wise man will hear and increase in learning". We should always get input from other people on the job if we want to learn. Or I also like the saying from the book of Ecclesiastes10:10 where it states: "A dull axe requires great strength, be wise and sharpen the blade". It always pays great rewards if we work smart and not just long hours.

JESUS ON FOCUS

Jesus knew exactly why He had come to planet earth as a human being. In the book of John 18:37 Jesus said: "In fact, for this reason I was born, and for this I came into the world, to testify to the truth". When you clearly know your objective and purpose, it enables you to focus. Jesus' whole life was dedicated to sharing critical truths. In Matthew 22:26 Jesus said: "What good will it be for a man if he gains the whole world, yet forfeits his soul?" On one occasion Jesus was asked which is the greatest commandment given by God. In Matthew 22:27 Jesus replied: "Love the Lord your God with all your heart and with all your soul and with all your mind". On another occasion Jesus said in Matthew 13:45: "Again, the kingdom of heaven is like a merchant looking for fine pearls. When he found one of great value, he went away and sold everything he had and bought it." Jesus' focus was to tell us that our focus needs to be on God and obeying His loving directions. In Matthew 9:35 the Bible says: "Jesus went through all of the towns and villages, teaching in their synagogues, preaching the good news of the kingdom." In Matthew 6:24 Jesus did have a serious warning for us about focus: "No one can serve two masters. Either he will hate the one and love the other, or he will be devoted to the one and despise the other. You cannot serve both God and money." He was not saying that money is evil, but rather that it is simply less important than God. In Matthew 6:23 Jesus said: "But seek first His kingdom and righteousness, and all these things will be given to you as well."

Jesus of course knew human nature, and He knew that many of us would not want to listen to His message. In Matthew 10:14 He said to His followers: "If anyone will not welcome you or listen to your words, shake off the dust from your feet when you leave that home or town." Jesus was telling His followers that it was their focus to go out and share the truths about God. But if some people would not listen to the truth, then they needed to leave and find another home where they were welcome. God created human beings with free will. He will not force us to focus on Him and live in a close relationship with Him. But God does want everyone to hear the truth and make a decision about Him.

NEHEMIAH ON WORK

One of my favorite books in the Bible about the topic of work is Nehemiah. He was employed as a high official in the court of the king of Babylon when he heard about the plight of the Jews in the conquered city of Jerusalem. Let's take a look at how Nehemiah lived out our various management principles for success.

Nehemiah was a man of great integrity. For example he honestly told the king that he wanted to go to Jerusalem to rebuild the city. He knew that the king could literally take off his head for such an unanticipated request. Nehemiah was afraid of what the king might do to him. But despite his fears, which we all have from time to time, Nehemiah spoke truth to the king in a straight forward manner. This example is exactly how we should relate to our manager at work.

Nehemiah's character is clearly on display as he interacts with the various people on the job. He was a man of humility. When he first arrived in Jerusalem, he kept a low profile. He asked the people what they needed, and how he should proceed with the rebuilding plans. He was friendly and open with his fellow workers. He communicated his decisions and plans in a clear manner. When he was questioned by the people, he gave them more details. When troubles arose on the job, he quickly addressed the issues. He often was working side by side with other team members so he understood the issues clearly. With his enemies he was tough and unwavering. Even they had a great deal of respect for Nehemiah.

I believe that Nehemiah's middle name was 'aggressive'. He wanted to rebuild the city walls as quickly as possible for protection against possible attacks. When some of his fellow workers were lazy on the job, he confronted them outwardly. And Nehemiah was very smart. He did not over extend his team during the work. He made sure that they had the resources necessary to finish the job. He also knew what he didn't know. When he first arrived in the city, he quietly went out to survey the demolished city walls. It was only after that fact finding trip that he formulated his plans for the work ahead.

Nehemiah managed to keep his project as simple as possible. His organization structure was very straight forward. Families were assigned to rebuild the part of the city wall that was right next to their homes. People were very motivated to protect their homes and families. Everyone had a clear job responsibility.

Nehemiah's focus was like a laser. When his enemies called upon him for a series of meetings, he said: "no". He said that he was too busy to be attending pointless meetings. That philosophy sounds perfect to me!

Nehemiah did his measuring by MBWA (management by walking around). He could readily see how high the wall was progressing in different parts of the city. Even more important, he was able to talk with people and assess their morale. He also periodically called meetings with his leaders to get their accurate reports. When there were issues identified in these reports, Nehemiah took decisive action.

Nehemiah knew that the people were his best asset. When some of the people fell down on the job, he tried to lift them up with consistent encouragement. In a few cases for the sake of the greater good of the people, he fired several leaders. When these leaders failed him, he conducted a public confrontation. It was clear to the workers that these few leaders had let them down, and action was necessary. Nehemiah was an effective leader.

Finally, and most important, Nehemiah was a prayer warrior. He knew that without God the work was doomed to failure. So for those of you who are Christian, I'd like to add one more key management principle: prayer. My wife and I start most mornings with a time of prayer. I simply ask God for His guidance and wisdom in my life. I ask God to lead me in a direction according to His will for me. If there is something that I want, I ask God to 'close doors' and block me, if it's not His will for my life. It's very reassuring to know that if I'm in God's will, then He is on my side. Or, I should say that I'm on His side. The bottom line is that I know that my God is far wiser than myself, and letting Him control my decisions will lead to far better results for me. It gives me great confidence and peace to walk with my almighty God.

PROVERBS ON LIFE

The book of Proverbs is full of hundreds of great words of wisdom for life. I'd like to quote several of them that apply especially well to a work situation.

Integrity:

The man of integrity walks securely. (10:9)

Do not accuse a man for no reason when he has done you no harm. (3:30)

Ill-gotten treasures are of no value. (10:2)

An evil man is trapped by his sinful talk. (12:13)

Kings take pleasure in honest lips; they value a man who speaks the truth. (16:13)

Humility:

Discretion will protect you, and understanding will guard you. (2:11)

He mocks proud mockers but gives grace to the humble. (3:34)

A fool shows his annoyance at once, but a prudent man overlooks an insult. (12:16)

Be Aggressive:

Wisdom is supreme; therefore get wisdom. Though it cost you all you have, get understanding. (4:7)

Whoever ignores correction leads others astray. (10:17)

It is not good to have zeal without knowledge. (19:2)

Keep It Simple:

A man of understanding keeps a straight course. (15:21)

Focus:

Let your eyes look straight ahead, fix your gaze directly before you. (4:25)

He who works his land will have abundant food, but he who chases fantasies lacks judgment. (12:11)

Measure It:

A simple man believes anything, but a prudent man gives thought to his steps. (14:15)

He who hates correction is stupid. (12:1)

The first to present his case seems right, till another comes forward and questions him. (18:17)

People:

He who walks with the wise grows wise, but a companion of fools suffers harm. (13:20)

Do not withhold good from those who deserve it, when it is in your power to act. (3:27)

Rebuke a wise man and he will love you. (9:8)

Honor the Lord with your wealth,...then your barns will be overflowing... (3:9)

NOTES

[1] Forbes Magazine editorial; February, 2009.

[2] Information Week editorial; Rob Preston; November 24, 2008.

[3] Senior Pastor David Sawkins; 2009.

[4] Predictably Irrational; Dan Ariely; 2008.

[5] Difficult Conversations; Douglas Stone, et al; 1999.

[6] Peopleware; Tom DeMarco, et al; 1987.

[7] Columbia Accident Investigation Board Report Volume 1; August, 2003.

[8] Information Week; Dr Dobbs Report; September, 2009.

[9] Leadership News Letter; Arlen Burger; July, 2009.

[10] The Case For Christ; Lee Strobel; 1998.

[11] www.meant4more.com; Web site owned by Global Media Outreach.

About The Author

Richard Sevcik was born in Chicago. He's the product of a strong Catholic elementary and high school training. Rich graduated as a James Scholar, Magna Cum Laude from the University of Illinois, BS in Engineering Physics with a major in mathematics. He was granted his Master's Degree in Electrical Engineering from Northwestern University. Rich was employed for ten years at AT&T, Bell Laboratories. He worked as a digital circuit designer and software engineer. He participated in the first telephone cell phone trial in Oak Park, Illinois. Rich then moved to California and joined Bell Northern Research, Northern Telecom. As a vice president he led the development of the Meridian Office Communication System, which achieved number one market share during the 1980's. After eight years Rich joined Hewlett Packard's computer organization. Again as vice president, group general manager he led a team of two thousand engineers in the development of HP's computer servers, workstations, and networking systems. HP's compute servers still enjoy a number one market share worldwide. Finally after ten years Rich joined Xilinx in the programmable logic industry. As executive vice president he led the development of Xilinx' ISE customer software tools, plus the Virtex and Spartan semiconductor product lines. Both of these product lines became number one in market share with the company exceeding $1.7 billion in revenue with more than 20% net income.

Currently Rich is retired from full time employment. He does consulting work part time including one Board seat. Rich and his wife also lead a Christian ministry called God Talk, speaking with un-churched people about God at local retail malls. (For more information go to www.Godtalkinthemall. com.)

You can be a leader with

Character

Plus

Common Sense!

"This book strikes me as the honorable man's 'how to guide' to success in management. I was also impressed with how the lessons that are good for management are also good for success in life." —Gary Meyers, Vice-President, Synopsys Corporation

"This book is a wonderful blending of management and Biblical principles. I strongly recommend it as a 'must read' for everyone in a leadership position." –David Sawkins, President of DS-Ministries

"Whether you are a CEO or the leader of your home, this book can empower you to be successful." —Kapil Shankar, CEO, Silicon Blue Technology

Breinigsville, PA USA
08 October 2010

246998BV00001B/6/P